بِسْمِ اللهِ الرَّحْمٰنِ الرَّحِيْمِ

All praise be to Allah subhanahu wa ta'ala (swt) and peace and blessings be upon our beloved prophet Muhammad ﷺ.
I hope that Allah (swt) will accept this work as Sadaqah Jariyah from myself and all those who contributed.

I would firstly like to thank my wonderful husband Rashad who has encouraged me from the day I proposed the
idea for this book 5 years ago and my parents and family who I can never repay for all they have given me.
May Allah (swt) grant them all a place in Jannat-Ul-Firdous in the next life.
The greatest of thanks to my mum Shameem who looked after Inaayah and Aisha so I could draw and paint
without too much disturbance! A special thank you to Awais, Hamza, Kosar and Sobiah for helping me find words
for the trickiest letters. A very special thanks to my sister Samina for helping me with the creation drawing;
my friend Umm Hamza for writing the Arabic for the Qur'an image (and others that didn't make the final version)
and my daughter Inaayah for illustrating a loving family.
Thank you to my Photoshop experts Ahmad and Omar for giving me your precious time and teaching me.
Thanks also to Ahmad and Shameq for helping me write the Arabic text.
Thank you to my baby Inaayah for drawing, painting and proof-reading for errors. If it wasn't for you we would
all be eating in Ramadhan when the sun was out!
Thanks to everyone who reviewed the book for me countless times and gave excellent suggestions for improvements.
There are too many of you to name and I would not want to miss anyone out!
Final thanks to Suhayl for giving me lots of guidance and information about the best printing options for this book.
Jazak'Allah Khair to you all.

May Allah (swt) bestow His peace and blessings on us all and help our children to grow and be beacons of light in
this world and inhabitants of Jannah in the next.   Ameen

Please visit www.auntiebstreasures.com for more
wonderful books, toys and resources for all the family!

For Inaayah, Aisha, Umaymah and Hanna
With love for my mum

Published by Islamic Beginnings 2018
Email: enquiries@islamicbeginnings.com
Text and illustration copyright © Bushra Taslim 2018
Moral rights asserted.

ISBN 978-1-9165014-0-9

A CIP catalogue record of this book is available from the British Library.

The illustrations in this book are drawn in black ink and painted with watercolour paints and watercolour pencils. The English font used is Schoolbell. The Arabic font used is Calibri.

Printed in the UK.

Islamic Beginnings

www.islamicbeginnings.com   www.auntiebstreasures.com

My Islam A-Z

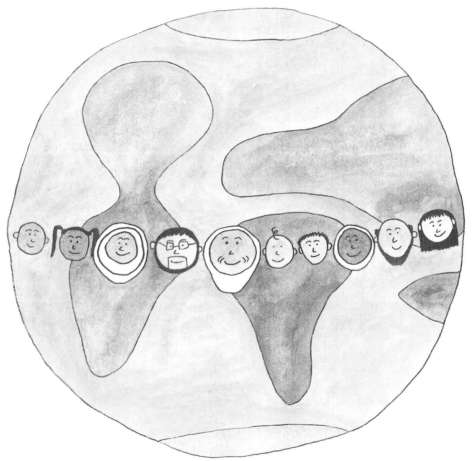

Bushra Taslim Hussain

A is for

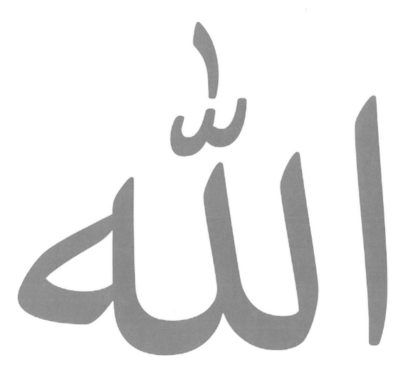

Allah

(God)

B is for

بِسْمِ اللهِ الرَّحْمٰنِ الرَّحِيْمِ

In the name of Allah,
the most Beneficent, the most Merciful

Bismillah

C is for

Creation

D is for

Du'a

(Supplication)

E is for

'Eid

(Muslim celebration)

F is for

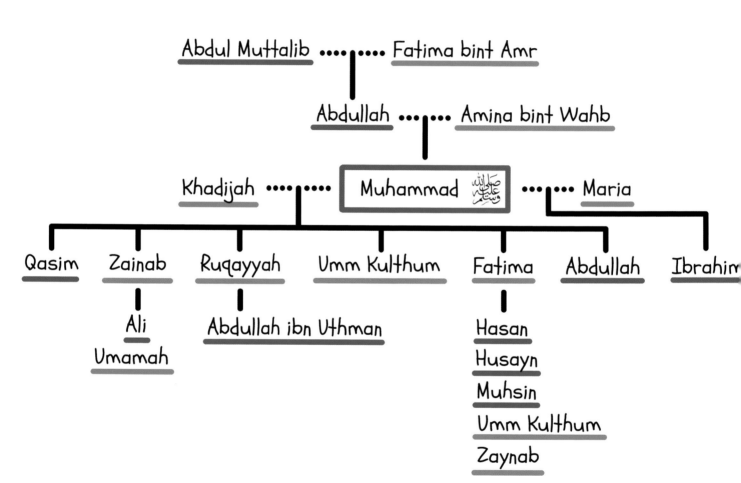

Abdul Muttalib ⋯⋯ **Fatima bint Amr**

Abdullah ⋯⋯ **Amina bint Wahb**

Khadijah ⋯⋯ **Muhammad** ﷺ ⋯⋯ **Maria**

Qasim   **Zainab**   **Ruqayyah**   **Umm Kulthum**   **Fatima**   **Abdullah**   **Ibrahim**

Ali

Abdullah ibn Uthman

Hasan

Umamah

Husayn

Muhsin

Umm Kulthum

Zaynab

Family

Peace and blessings of Allah be upon them all

G is for

Love   Smile

Help 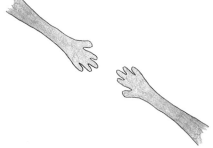 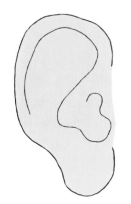 Listen

Good deeds

H is for

1. Meeqat
(Place where pilgrims
enter the state of Ihram)

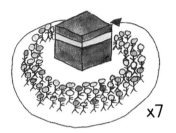

2. Tawaaf
(Circling the Ka'bah)

3. Drinking Zamzam

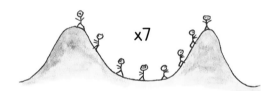

4. Sa'i between Safa and Marwa
(Running between Safa and Marwa)

5. Praying at Mount Arafat

6. Jamarat
(Stoning Pillars)

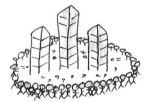

7. Qurbani
(Sacrifice)

Hajj
(Pilgrimage)

I is for

Islam

(Physical and spiritual submission to the Will of Allah)

J is for

Jannah

(Heaven)

K is for

Ka'bah

L is for

لَا إِلٰهَ إِلَّا اللهُ

مُحَمَّدٌ رَّسُوْلُ اللهِ

There is no God but Allah
Muhammad (peace be upon him) is His messenger

La ilaha illallah
Muhammadur Rasulullah ﷺ

M is for

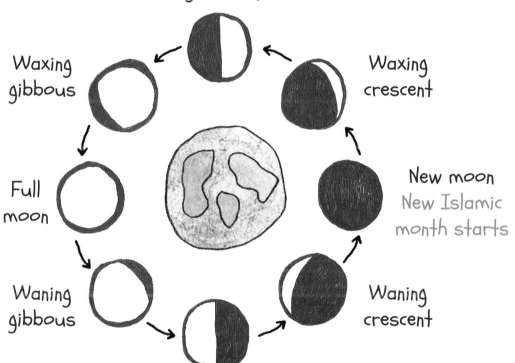

Waxing first quarter

Waxing gibbous

Waxing crescent

Waxing crescent

Full moon

New moon

New Islamic month starts

Waning gibbous

Waning crescent

Waning last quarter

Moon

N is for

Reward for a good deed

JANNAH POINT   JANNAH POINT   JANNAH POINT

Reward for same good deed
with intention of pleasing Allah

JANNAH POINT   JANNAH POINT   JANNAH POINT

JANNAH POINT   JANNAH POINT   JANNAH POINT

JANNAH POINT   JANNAH POINT   JANNAH POINT

Niyyah
(Intention)

O is for

Olives

P is for

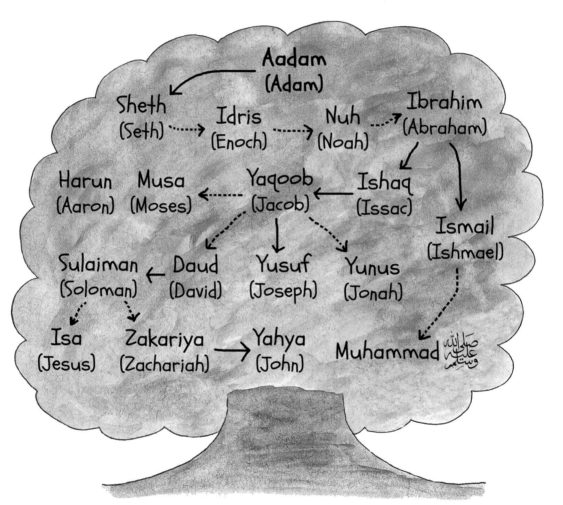

Prophets

Peace and blessings of Allah be upon them all

Q is for

Qur'an

R is for

Ramadhan

S is for

Salah

(Prayer)

T is for

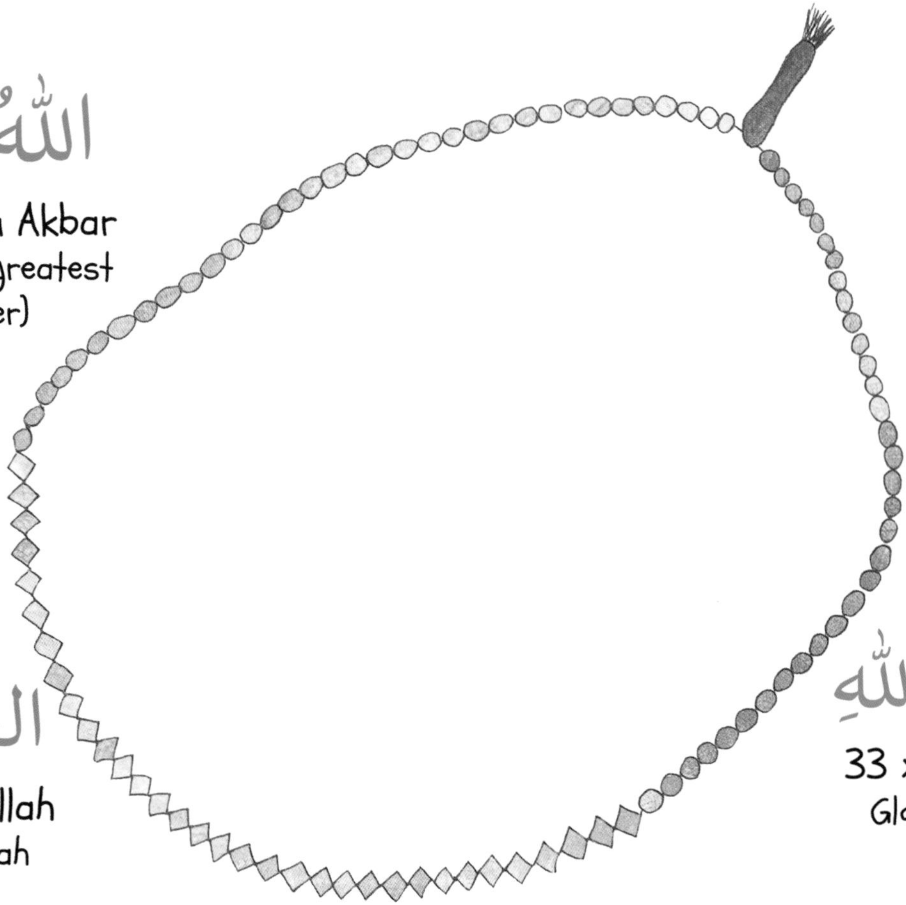

الله أَكْبَرُ

34 x Allahu Akbar
Allah is the greatest
(Takbeer)

سُبْحَانَ اللهِ

33 x Subhan Allah
Glory be to Allah
(Tasbeeh)

الحَمْدُ لِلّهِ

33 x Alhamdulillah
Praise be to Allah
(Tahmid)

Tasbeeh

U is for

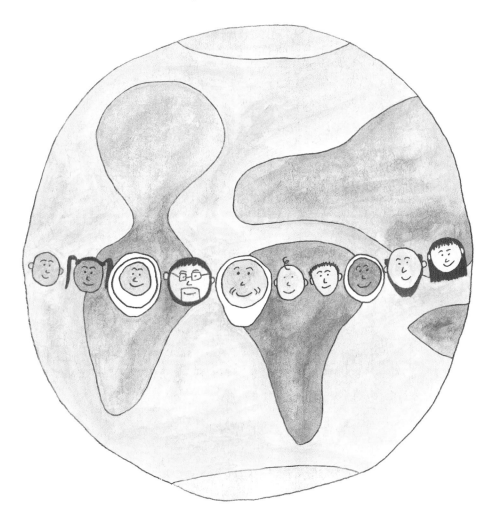

Ummah

(Community)

V is for

Visiting the sick

W is for

1. Hands x3

2. Inside of mouth x3

3. Nose x3

4. Face x3

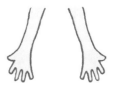
5. Arms x3

6. Hair, neck and ears x1

7. Feet x3

Wudhu
(Washing for prayer)

X is for

Best Effort

eXcellence

Y is for

Yawm al Qiyamah

(Day of Judgement)

Z is for

Zakah

(Obligatory Charity)

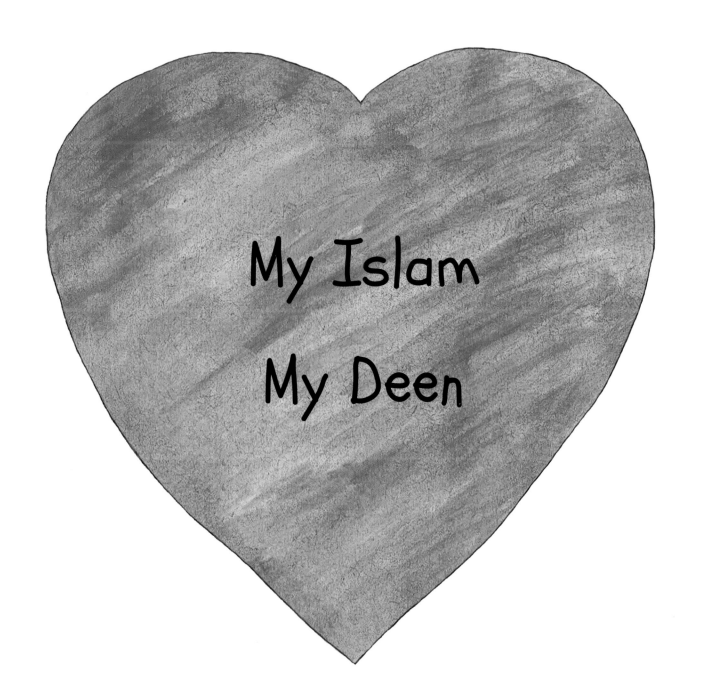

Glossary

Allah: The Arabic word for God.

Bismillah hir-Rahman nir-Raheem: Muslims say this phrase before starting anything.

Deen: The Arabic word for faith and religion.

Du'a: A special prayer to Allah to thank Him for all His blessings and to ask for good things and forgiveness for any bad deeds.

Eid: There are two eids. Eid-ul-Fitr is the celebration that marks the end of Ramadhan. Eid-ul-Adha celebrates the completion of the Hajj.

Hajj: One of the five pillars of Islam. It is a once in a lifetime requirement for Muslims to go on the pilgrimage to Makkah if they are able to.

Ihram: The physical/spiritual state that pilgrims enter when they reach the boundary of Makkah.

Islam: Islam means submission, specifically relating to submitting oneself to the will of Allah (God).

Jannah: The Arabic word for heaven. This is where all Muslims wish to go to in the Hereafter.

Ka'bah: The first masjid built by Adam and re-built by Ibrahim (Abraham) and his son Ismail (Ishmael) in Makkah. Muslims face the Ka'bah when they pray salah 5 times a day.

Masjid: The name for the place of worship for Muslims.

Niyyah: The Arabic word for intention. In Islam, you are rewarded for your actions based on your intention. The greater the intention, the greater the reward even for the same action.

Qur'an: The direct word of Allah sent as guidance for all of mankind.

Ramadhan: The ninth month of the Islamic calendar where all healthy, adult Muslims fast from dawn to sunset. This includes all food and drinks, even water.

Salah: One of the five pillars of Islam. There are five daily prayers: Fajr (before sunrise), Dhuhr (after midday), Asr (late afternoon), Maghrib (after sunset) and Isha (night).

Sawm: One of the five pillars of Islam. Sawm means to fast from all food and water during daylight hours. Muslims fast in Ramadhan for 29 or 30 days depending on the lunar cycle.

Shahadah: One of the five pillars of Islam. This is a declaration of faith that a Muslim believes in Allah and that Muhammad (peace be upon him) is the final messenger.

Tasbeeh: Recitation of specific phrases to glorify, remember and praise Allah.

Ummah: The Arabic word for community.

Wudhu: The ritual washing to cleanse oneself before acts of worship such as offering salah.

Yawm al Qiyamah: The Arabic words for the Day of Judgement where all deeds are accounted for.

Zakah: One of the five pillars of Islam. An obligatory act of purification of wealth by giving a minimum of 2.5% of a person's saved annual wealth to those who are eligible to receive Zakah.